I0473604

120-page Music manuscript book

Melbourne 2014

ISBN 978-0-9924332-2-2

1		
2		
3		
4		
5		
6		
7		
8		
9		
10		
11		
12		
13		
14		
15		
16		
17		
18		
19		
20		
21		
22		
23		
24		
25		
26		
27		
28		
29		
30		
31		
32		
33		
34		
35		
36		
37		
38		
39		
40		

41		
42		
43		
44		
45		
46		
47		
48		
49		
50		
51		
52		
53		
54		
55		
56		
57		
58		
59		
60		
61		
62		
63		
64		
65		
66		
67		
68		
69		
70		
71		
72		
73		
74		
75		
76		
77		
78		
79		
80		

81		
82		
83		
84		
85		
86		
87		
88		
89		
90		
91		
92		
93		
94		
95		
96		
97		
98		
99		
100		
101		
102		
103		
104		
105		
106		
107		
108		
109		
110		
111		
112		
113		
114		
115		
116		
117		
118		
119		
120		

www.ingramcontent.com/pod-product-compliance
Lightning Source LLC
Chambersburg PA
CBHW081047170526
45158CB00006B/1889
* 9 7 8 0 9 9 2 4 3 3 2 2 2 *